A HERITAGE & FAMILY DESIGNED BY GOD

WORKING TO RESTORE FAMILY ORDER

BY

TONYA HAUGABROOK

A Goshen Publishers Book

A Heritage & Family Designed by God
ISBN: 978-1-7370949-4-4

Copyright ©2021 Tonya Haugabrook

Library of Congress Cataloging-in-Publication Data

Published in 2021 by:

GOSHEN PUBLISHERS LLC
P.O. Box 1562
Stephens City, Virginia, USA
www.GoshenPublishers.com

Our books may be purchased in bulk for promotional, educational, or business use. For inquiries please contact the publisher via email: Agents@GoshenPublishers.com.

Published in 2004 by The Right Start Publishers. Reprinted by Nehemiah's Vision in 2009.

Third Edition 2021

Cover designed by Goshen Publishers LLC

Printed in the United States of America

All Scriptures are quoted from the King James translation of the Bible unless otherwise noted. Scripture quotations noted LB are from the Living Bible. Scriptures noted NIV are from the New International Version. All rights reserved.

A HERITAGE & FAMILY DESIGNED BY GOD

WORKING TO RESTORE FAMILY ORDER

TONYA HAUGABROOK

DEDICATION

To my Lord and Savior, Jesus Christ: all that I am or ever hope to be, I owe it all to you. To God Be All the Glory!

To my children: a mother could not ask for three more loving and supportive kids. I am truly blessed for having you in my life.

To my parents: in your own way, you taught me to be strong and believe I could achieve my dreams.

To my sisters and brother: although we do not always see eye-to-eye, there is one thing we have always shared. That is our love for one another. I thank God that after all these years, I can still look to you and say you are not only my siblings, but also my friends.

To all my wonderful friends: thank you for being there for me when things seemed hopeless. You will never know how much your many words of encouragement and prayers meant to me.

INTRODUCTION

Abram came from what we today would call a rich and privileged heritage. He was born of the ninth generation of Shem, son of Noah. He had a close-knit family, which was evident by how the family became a father unto Lot after the death of his father (Abram's youngest brother).

Yet despite his rich heritage, God had a plan for Abram to begin a new family and heritage designed to bring Him glory, honor and praise — one that would worship Him as God alone.

Abram would have missed out on this godly designed family and heritage had he not done three things: leave a land of sin and idolatry, believe that God is faithful to fulfill His promises, and cleave to the commandments of God.

Even today, God is constantly calling us. He is calling us to leave a life of sin; calling us to believe His promises of life and prosperity. He is calling us to obey His commandments so that He can bless us. God's promises to His children are just as good today as they were in Abram's day. We must, like Abram, move in the direction that God is leading in order to receive the blessings He has preordained for us.

CONTENTS

1.

SIN AND IDOLATRY

Let us begin by examining Abram.

> 1 Now the LORD had said unto Abram, "Get thee out of thy country, and from thy kindred, and from thy father's house, unto a land that I will shew thee:
>
> 2 And I will make of thee a great nation, and I will bless thee, and make thy name great; and thou shalt be a blessing:
>
> 3 And I will bless them that bless thee, and curse him that curseth thee: and in thee shall all families of the earth be blessed."
>
> Genesis 12:1-3

We all know the outcome of Abram's blessing from God. He became the father of the nation of Israel. He amassed great wealth. And, he was counted as a friend of God. That outcome was not immediately evident to Abram when God first spoke to him as Abram and told him to leave his country, his kindred, and his father's house, and go to an unknown land (Genesis 12:1).

You may ask what is the big deal about leaving these things behind? Abram was a grown man with a wife.

Why was he not out there building a name for himself instead of staying in the shadow of his father's name?

It was customarily recognized in those days that a man's country, his kindred, and his father's house were directly associated with his social status in the community. There are so many examples in the Bible where instead of just saying the person's name you see something like "James son of ... (the father's name)" to clearly identify James. An example is in Mark 3:17a, "And James the son of Zebedee".

So, when God told Abram to leave his father's house, He was in turn telling Abram to leave the heritage (societal identity) passed onto him from his forefathers and in turn accept a new country and family name that no one knew.

Now, contrary to how society thinks today, Abram was not trying to move far away from his family to become a great nation or build a great name. This was God's plan and purpose for Abram's life.

Abram was content with following the tradition of his time, which was to stay in his father's house and live in a familial land. Also, it was customarily acceptable for a family to stay together for protection. That was clearly shown when Lot's father died (Genesis 11:28).

So, we also see that by obeying God's command Abram would leave the protection that was believed to be found within the family circle. But why would God ask Abram to make such a drastic move before he could receive his blessing?

When Abram's father Terah moved Abram (then Abram), his wife Sarah (then Sarai), and nephew Lot to a new land, they settled in Haran. Haran was the ancient city of Mesopotamia, an important trade route and the chief center of worship of the Assyrian moon god. Idolatry was heavily practiced in that land, yet this was Abram's country and the place of dwelling with his father. God knew that in order to bless Abram he would have to break that link with a country that worshipped idols.

Why? God is Holy and although the Ten Commandments had not yet been written for man's reading, God had already spoken in the spiritual realm that "Thou shalt have no other gods before me" (Exodus 20:3).

God had already made examples of those that tried to exalt themselves above Him. He cast Lucifer out of heaven (Isaiah 14:12; Luke 10:18; Revelation 12:9). He sent the great floods on the earth and spared only Noah and his family (Genesis 7:1; 2 Peter 2:5). He confused the builders of the tower of Babel when they attempted to build a tower to heaven thinking they could share God's throne (Genesis 11:1-9). In each example, they all learned that God reigns supreme and will not bless that which is unholy.

God was looking for a faithful man whom He could choose to become the father of a nation that would begin a new heritage of worshippers and He found that in Abram.

I ask you today, what type of heritage are you building for your family? Is it a heritage that will bring God glory and honor? Does it teach your children to put God first in all they do? Does it encourage them to develop a personal relationship with God and learn His ways and statutes? Does it make demons fear each morning when you rise, or does it have Satan and his angels dancing for joy knowing they will be amused by your daily antics?

> 18 Seeing that Abraham shall surely become a great and mighty nation, and all the nations of the earth shall be blessed in him?
>
> 19 For I know him, that he will command his children and his household after him, and they shall keep the way of the Lord, to do justice and judgment; that the Lord may bring upon Abraham that which he hath spoken of him.
>
> Genesis 18:18-19

When you refuse to leave behind a lifestyle that is unpleasing to God, you block the blessings that God wants to bestow upon you and your children. Herein, you begin a generational curse that will only be destroyed by one person making the decision to return to God.

> And to Seth, to him also there was born a son; and he called his name Enos: then began men to call upon the name of the Lord.
>
> Genesis 4:26

> 1 And it shall come to pass, if thou shalt hearken diligently unto the voice of the LORD thy God, to observe and to do all his commandments which I command thee this day, that the LORD thy God will set thee on high above all nations of the earth:
>
> 2 And all these blessings shall come on thee, and overtake thee, if thou shalt hearken unto the voice of the LORD thy God.
>
> Deuteronomy 28:1-2

When you refuse to live holy before God, you lay a foundation for your children that is not built on Godly principles. Thus, you force God to close His ears to your cries and prayers and consequently, you open your entire household and generations to come under God's wrath.

> 13 And this again you do. You cover the LORD's altar with tears, with weeping and groaning because he no longer regards the offering or accepts it with favor at your hand.
>
> 14 You ask, "Why does he not?" Because the LORD was witness to the covenant between you and the wife of your youth, to whom you have been faithless, though she is your companion and your wife by covenant.
>
> 15 Has not the one God made and sustained for us the spirit of life? And what does he desire? Godly offspring. So take heed to yourselves, and let none be faithless to the wife of his youth."
>
> Malachi 3:13-15

> 3 And say thou unto them, Thus saith the LORD God of Israel; "Cursed be the man that obeyeth not the words of this covenant."
>
> Jeremiah 11:3

> 5 Mortify therefore your members which are upon the earth; fornication,

uncleanness, inordinate affection, evil concupiscence, and covetousness, which is idolatry:

6 For which things' sake the wrath of God cometh on the children of disobedience:
Colossians 3:5-6

15 But it shall come to pass, if thou wilt not hearken unto the voice of the LORD thy God, to observe to do all his commandments and his statutes which I command thee this day; that all these curses shall come upon thee, and overtake thee:
Deuteronomy 28:15

So, the first step in moving your family toward a heritage designed by God is to commit in your heart to leave behind the sins that will keep your family from receiving the full blessings of God and begin walking toward a new country (a new lifestyle) that will allow your family to inherit the same blessings and promises of Abram.

7 Know ye therefore that they which are of faith, the same are the children of Abram.

8 And the scripture, foreseeing that God would justify the heathen through faith, preached before the gospel unto Abram, saying, In thee shall all nations be blessed.

9 So then they which be of faith are blessed with faithful Abram.

Galatians 3:7-9

2.

FAITH AND PROMISES

Now that you understand why it is important to leave the world of sin and idolatry, we can move on to the next step.

The second step to having a heritage and family designed by God is to believe that God is faithful.

> 1 After these things the word of the LORD came unto Abram in a vision, saying, Fear not, Abram: I am thy shield, and thy exceeding great reward.
>
> 2 And Abram said, LORD God, what wilt thou give me, seeing I go childless, and the steward of my house is this Eliezer of Damascus?
>
> 3 And Abram said, Behold, to me thou hast given no seed: and, lo, one born in my house is mine heir.
>
> 4 And, behold, the word of the LORD came unto him, saying, This shall not be thine heir; but he that shall come forth out of thine own bowels shall be thine heir.
>
> 5 And he brought him forth abroad, and said, "Look now toward heaven, and tell the stars, if thou be able to number them:

and he said unto him, So shall thy seed be."

6 And he believed in the LORD; and he counted it to him for righteousness.

Genesis 15:1-6

God is seeking men and women who are willing to believe His promises of generational blessings are true. We see in Genesis (chapter 15) that Abram was told of a promise that would not be manifested for four generations, which meant Abram would neither see nor experience this blessing. Despite knowing this, Abram did not consider seeking his own pleasures in life. Instead, he stood firm on God's promises for his future generations.

15 And thou shalt go to thy fathers in peace; thou shalt be buried in a good old age.

16 But in the fourth generation they shall come hither again: for the iniquity of the Amorites is not yet full.

Genesis 15:15-16

No wonder God credited Abram's belief as righteousness. The promise was more than 200 years in the future so Abram had no choice but to believe that God would honor His promise long after he was dead.

Are you willing to believe God like Abram for the future of your family? Are you teaching your children Godly principles so they will be blessed for generations to come or are you seeking your own wealth and leaving the teaching of Godly principles up to the scientists, education professionals, child experts, television ministers and talk show hosts?

When you choose to walk holy before God, you are leaving Haran and entering the land of promise. Like Abram, you will make choices that will affect your family for generations to come. You can follow the example of Abram and your family will be blessed according to God's promises or you can reject God and open your family to curses. Years later, we see how Abram's belief paved the way for Joshua, David, and others to stand when their trust in God was challenged.

> 14 Now therefore fear the Lord, and serve him in sincerity and in truth: and put away the gods, which your fathers served on the other side of the flood, and in Egypt; and serve ye the Lord.
>
> 15 And if it seem evil unto you to serve the LORD, choose you this day whom ye will serve; whether the gods which your fathers served that were on the other side of the flood, or the gods of the Amorites, in whose land ye dwell: but as for me and my house, we will serve the LORD.
>
> *Joshua 24:14-15*

When you believe God, you are committed in your heart to living a holy lifestyle that gives Him praise.

Him: He is the author and finisher of your faith (Hebrews 12:2).

Him: Jehovah Jireh, the God of provision (Genesis 22:14). He will provide your family's every need.

Him: Jehovah Shalom, the God of peace (Judges 6:24). He will give your family a peace that will strengthen and keep them in times of trouble.

Him: Jehovah Shammah, God thy healer (Ezekiel 48:35). No matter what the diagnosis He is able to heal your family and restore them to complete health.

Him: Jehovah Nissim, God thy Banner (Exodus 17:15). God will fight every battle your family encounters and always make them victorious.

I am sure these are promises we all want for our family. However, we must remember that believing God is not an option for receiving these promises, it is the requirement. There is no such thing as negotiating or brokering a deal with God. Either you trust Him for His Word, or you do not. You cannot be lukewarm in your belief and stance. You must be either hot or cold.

> *So then because thou art lukewarm, and neither cold nor hot, I will spue thee out of my mouth.*
>
> *Revelation 3:16*

12 And now, Israel, what doth the LORD thy God require of thee, but to fear the LORD thy God, to walk in all his ways, and to love him, and to serve the LORD thy God with all thy heart and with all thy soul,

13 To keep the commandments of the LORD, and his statutes, which I command thee this day for thy good?

14 Behold, the heaven and the heaven of heavens is the LORD's thy God, the earth also, with all that therein is.

15 Only the LORD had a delight in thy fathers to love them, and he chose their seed after them, even you above all people, as it is this day.

Deuteronomy 10:12-15

So the second step to moving your family toward a heritage designed by God is to believe God is faithful and His promises are true.

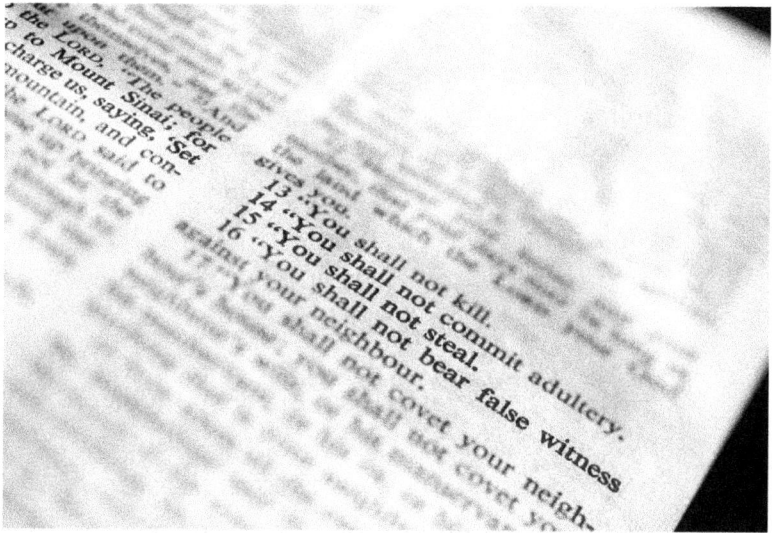

3·

COMMANDMENTS

The last step in establishing a family and heritage designed by God is to cleave to God's Word.

> *20 Thou shalt fear the LORD thy God; him shalt thou serve, and to him shalt thou cleave, and swear by his name.*
>
> *21 He is thy praise, and he is thy God, that hath done for thee these great and terrible things, which thine eyes have seen.*
>
> *22 Thy fathers went down into Egypt with threescore and ten persons; and now the LORD thy God hath made thee as the stars of heaven for multitude.*
>
> Deuteronomy 10:20-22

God's Word is our instruction book for living. Therefore, it is impossible to live a life that will move God to bless your family when you refuse to cleave to His Word. The Old Testament as well as the New Testament encourages us to cleave to God's Word.

> *15 Study to shew thyself approved unto God, a workman that needeth not to be ashamed, rightly dividing the word of truth.*
>
> 2 Timothy 2:15

14 And above all these put on love, which binds everything together in perfect harmony.

15 And let the peace of Christ rule in your hearts, to which indeed you were called in the one body. And be thankful.

16 Let the word of Christ dwell in you richly, teach and admonish one another in all wisdom, and singing psalms and hymns and spiritual songs, with thankfulness in your hearts to God.

17 And whatever you do, in word or deed, do everything in the name of the Lord Jesus, giving thanks to God the Father through him.

Colossians 3:14-17, ESV

Therefore put away all filthiness and rampant wickedness and receive with meekness the implanted word, which is able to save your souls.

James 1:21, ESV

12 For the word of God is living and powerful, and sharper than any two-edged sword, piercing even to the division of soul and spirit, and of joints and

*marrow, and is a discerner of the thoughts
and intents of the heart.*

*13 And there is no creature hidden from His
sight, but all things are naked and open to
the eyes of Him to whom we must give
account.*

Hebrews 4:12-13, ESV

*This book of the law shall not depart out
of thy mouth; but thou shalt meditate
therein day and night, that thou mayest
observe to do according to all that is
written therein: for then thou shalt make
thy way prosperous, and then thou shalt
have good success.*

Joshua 1:8

When you fail to cleave to God's Word you will find it
hard, if not impossible, to live holy before God.
Consequently, you will find yourself living a double
lifestyle and pass that lifestyle of struggling and
straddling the fence unto your children. They will pass
it on to their children until a generation produces one
person that is committed to living a life pleasing to
God.

When you cleave to God's Word then and only then will the Word become your instruction book for living, thereby establishing a heritage and family designed by God for generations to come.

> 5 But take diligent heed to do the commandment and the law, which Moses the servant of the LORD charged you, to love the LORD your God, and to walk in all his ways, and to keep his commandments, and to cleave unto him, and to serve him with all your heart and with all your soul.
>
> *Joshua 22:5, ESV*

When you are committed to reading, studying, and hiding God's Word in your heart, your love for God and His ways will grow. You will find yourself acknowledging God in all aspects of your life and thereby building a heritage for your family that will bring blessings for your children's children and more.

So the last step to moving your family toward a heritage designed by God is to cleave (live according) to God's Word.

God has always had one desire for his creation and that is to bless and prosper us. When we trust God's ultimate plan for our family, we will trust Him as Abram and receive the same promise given to Abram.

> *26 For you are all sons of God through faith in Christ Jesus.*
>
> *27 For as many of you as were baptized into Christ have put on Christ.*
>
> *28 There is neither Jew nor Greek, there is neither slave nor free, there is neither male nor female; for you are all one in Christ Jesus.*
>
> *29 And if you are Christ's, then you are Abram's seed, and heirs according to the promise.*
>
> Galatians 3:26-29, NKJV

Make the decision today to refuse living a life of mediocrity and open your heart to believe that the promises of Abram are for you and your family today.

I AM SOMEBODY

I am somebody someone said,
For I am a tall, strong, and prominent man;

I am somebody someone proclaimed,
For I have great wealth, fortune, and fame;

I am somebody someone roared,
For my race is superior, all other inferior;

I am somebody another said,
For I have come a long way,
And am now equal to man;

I am somebody and this I am sure,
It is not because of wealth or who,
I proclaim I am;

It is not because of my struggle,
or the color of my skin;

But I am somebody because I know,
I was made by the Hands of God,
An I am kept by His Love.

CONTACT THE AUTHOR

Tonya Haugabrook would love to know how her books bless you and your family.

Connect with her, invite her to your study group, follow her on social media, or purchase her other books at
GoshenPublishers.com/Tonya-Haugabrook.

May God bless you richly with the heritage and family that He designed.

www.ingramcontent.com/pod-product-compliance
Lightning Source LLC
Chambersburg PA
CBHW071458070426
42452CB00040B/1863